ALTERATIONS

CORI WINROCK

TRANSIT
BOOKS

Published by Transit Books
1250 Addison St #103, Berkeley, CA 94702
www.transitbooks.org

ISBN: 9798893389012 (paperback)
Cover design by Anna Morrison | Typesetting by Transit Books
Printed in the United States of America

9 8 7 6 5 4 3 2 1

To Gillian Paku+

And then there was Rose.+

Rose was her name and would she have been Rose if her name had not been Rose. She used to think and then she used to think again.

Would she have been Rose if her name had not been Rose and would she have been Rose if she had been a twin.

Rose was her name all the same—

GERTRUDE STEIN

The World Is Round

But if I put on a white dress and go out, I will be lost in the light—and lost again—and lost again in that slow leap to a higher plane—and how will I find the spring in my absence? Rosa, please iron my blackest dress.

CLARICE LISPECTOR

Too Much of Life: The Complete Crônicas

What is a +variation? It is an art and a risk.

ANNE DUFOURMANTELLE

In Praise of Risk

+a variant

Look closely at any moon-landing photograph and you will find fine gray plus signs in a grid across each one—plus signs that allowed for distortion to be corrected + for distance and height to be calibrated from space as well as on the moon's surface. That could stitch a panoramic sequence of images + plot the moon. Each Hasselblad camera the astronauts brought was fitted with a glass plate etched with this precise network, a réseau of stitches—pinning the moon to the moon to keep its surface and the vast black horizon in line. Réseau: a grid + a reference-marking pattern on a photograph or sewing paper + an intelligence network + a net of fine lines on glass plates + a foundation in lace.

Look closely at many Emily Dickinson poems and you will find + signs that indicate a variant in a line. A variant may appear + above a word + to the side of a line + underneath a word + at right angles to the poem + stacked at the end like a solution to an equation. Whole poems + sequences may be variants of each other. Dickinson did not choose among her variants, offering them as concurrent alternatives—evocative lace constellations left for us to hold up to our future sky as we try to align the wild nights + noons of her poems + epistolary impulses. Stitched across the surface of her work—plus signs that allow for + stray signals + distortion + that calibrate interior vastness.

I+

In the city where I was born there is a collective of women taking apart donated wedding dresses. Seam ripping and taking off lace, uprooting stitches and unstringing beads—one by one by hand in their spare time. All across the country there are similar knots of women reversing someone else's hours of meticulous handwork. These women are always looking for more women, particularly ones who would rather not+ sew, to help take the garments apart. They are looking for those of us with patience for+ something's undoing. Recently they were bequeathed a gown with an exceptionally long train, every inch covered in lace appliqué. Stitch after stitch as small as a sewing needle's eye. They say it takes a very long time to undo a dress like this. To carefully remove every thread.

+cannot

+reverence for +devotion to

As with many collectives whose existence and skills might seem unfathomable, most of us won't know about them until there is a need to know. Even then, I didn't know of them. I only know of them belatedly.

These women also look for people to collect dresses from their neighborhoods around town, for drivers to deliver the gowns. Every few months, the women then gather for a sew-in to +unsew, to replenish their supply of what is +undone. After an article appears in the local paper, they soon have an overly abundant archive of garments for taking apart. Too many to be useful. After all, a single unstitched dress can turn from one into so many. The women who need to know, or who have heard of women who need to know, continue to pull their wedding dresses from their closets.

+resew
+redone

+ The clothes that I prefer are those I
invent for a life that doesn't exist yet—
the world of tomorrow +

| +

Rather than the stunning aluminum-coated fabric of the *Mercury* crews stepping out of comic book frames of imagined interstellar travel, the astronauts who planted their feet on the moon were outfitted in the same glaring white as a wedding dress. A color that, in the future, will become as synonymous as silver with the zeitgeist of 1960s space-age fabrics—avant-garde apparel made of paper and metal and mirrors and all that lamé, every garment a mise en abyme reflecting and replicating a future possible. Silver and white, twin colors that wax and wane in popularity across time, reappearing again and again when we most need to transport ourselves beyond whatever present moment in which we find ourselves suspended. Colors that carry us across the thin gray twilight line that separates us from a speculative future.

> + Every pattern carries within it the potential garment and therefore, the potential body. +

Fifty years into that future, it's difficult to undo the images of those sonogramic white suits. The ghostly bulk of the astronauts' bodies adrift on the moon now an afterimage in our collective consciousness. The exterior garment as luminous and otherworldly + everyday and intimate as the era's conic Playtex bras. Fabric chosen in part for its superlative heat resistance, in part because its less reflective surface kept the astronauts safer from + the risk of dazzling themselves with their clothing while facing unfiltered sunlight. + Underneath this bright+ white micrometeoroid layer, underneath the layers and layers of nested silver insulation, the main pressurized body of the spacesuit is a simple Earthly blue.

+protective

|+

+ And I think I'd like to go into space. And I'd like to wear our own suit that we sew. I think I could depend on it. +

In 2014 an artist ties and weighs down a black wedding dress to the bottom of the Dead Sea. A sea which is actually a salt lake at the lowest place on Earth, rapidly evaporating off the map. The water's high salinity makes everything float. She has to keep it from bobbing to the surface as if coming up for air. Even just one dress requires a complex rig of ropes and weights and a crew to lower it into the water. And that one dress is already infamous. Modeled after one worn by Hanna Rovina as Leah in *The Dybbuk*, in the scene where the spirit of her dead beloved enters her body, taking over her soul before she can be wed to another. Night after night for almost forty years, Rovina's one white dress turning from bridal to black as she enters possessed for the last act. Until Rovina's + Leah's dress becomes part of a collective consciousness.

+ stitched with a netlike weave that
the sea would respond to +

For over three months the replica dress holds its breath, remaining submerged as saltwater washes through its fabric. Suspended from a metal frame that looks like a chuppah—as if the bride has evaporated, leaving an empty dress at the altar +on the seafloor. As the plain black gown is encased + into the white wedding dress it was always intended to be + the spirit of the dead remains underneath. A dress of mourning and a dress of marriage suspended together. Every thread and pleat duplicated in salt.

By then the hems are too stiff to drift, the dress so heavy it can't be dredged whole from the water. Sections of it keep breaking off in the sea.

+in her wake.

I +

+ Never Bride had such Assembling – +

The year we land on the moon a documentary is screened detailing the seemingly impossible technological processes involved in getting us there. Over looped footage—a modified sewing machine moving stitch over stitch over a seam—a sheet of mylar pulled from a roll until its silver fills the screen—a pair of gloves being constructed blue finger by finger—there is audio of women talking. Chatting back and forth with each other as if they are doing any day's work. What's hidden in this small loop is the intimacy of the moon landing: the spacesuits with their otherworldly specifications being sewn one by one.

The seamstresses hired to help fabricate the spacesuits first had to learn how to read blueprints, to understand construction and possible seam lines from engineering drawings rather than paper patterns or even a previous garment. There was no garment to take apart. No stitches to unpick or ghost with a tracing wheel, no way to learn where hidden seams and extra protection from friction might be required. No creases or details to close-read what happens to fabric on the body when worn on the moon, the intricacies or possible failures of a former design. The seamstresses had to sew the spacesuit together in their minds. Undo it to imagine it again as flat fabric. Understand how to cut + piece + dip + coat edges of ever more wild fabrics to keep them from fraying + tearing + coming undone in space while being worn.

Given the unfathomable demand for stitches so +meticulous they would allow a body to safely endure a lack of breathable air, the seamstresses learned to sew at a level of precision even the most spectacular Earth garment would never call for. They learned to sew with almost no use of straight pins to tack together their fabrics and keep them from slipping as layer after layer of delicate + fiberglass + heatproof fabric was run through the machine. That even a single misplaced stitch might call for a suit to be fully +restarted. Learned an errant pin and an infinitesimal hole in the pressurized suit were the only difference between—and—. And no Earthly rehearsal before the seamstresses' trick of turning flat fabric into an airtight heirloom was performed live by astronauts in front of a national audience.

+hermetic
+discarded

Pinned down in grief, and imagining I have landed on the moon, I hear them. Their voices bounced up fifty years in the future like stray signals through the night sky. As if I am overhearing a garment in process across multiple moments in time.

I +

+ Distance – be her only | + signal +

Earth—
How to make the moon come down to those of us still on Earth? Almost forty years after the last lunar astronauts hurtle in their impossibly stitched suits into + out of our night sky, an artist will transmit a morse code translation of the "Moonlight Sonata" 240,000 miles up to the moon's surface. A few seconds later it will bounce back—missing dots and dashes of the code. When retranscribed into musical notation, all those absences and pauses and spaces and hesitations—signals and notes lost in craters and the dust—turn the musical score into lace. Little +rents in the fabric of—. A musical rendition of moonlight,

altered by the moon. Each note not reflected is left to drift among the flags and discarded lunar landers, and the little thrown hammer and all those lost Hasselblad cameras—too heavy to risk bringing back on board.

+pinholes

Moon—
And how did we figure out the moon could reflect ourselves back to ourselves in the first place? Secret morse code messages meant for someone somewhere else are found bouncing off the moon's surface and back down to us on Earth. A constellation of dits and dahs that accidentally reaches the ears of an engineer who imagines the otherworldly possibility of overhearing these +stray signals. His curiosity turns the moon into an intelligence network, a réseau + a lacework allowing interception and communication between sea and space and shore. Operation Moon Bounce: the foundation to tracking and data relay satellites that people in the future will wish on by accident as if shooting stars.

+patterns

Earth—
And in a further future, when an Earth plague shuts us all inside, incubates our loneliness, people will again seek out this overhearing. Eavesdroppers and talkers alike tuning in and trawling, transmitting and trying to locate each other by reflecting their stories off the moon's cratered surface. Listening into the vastness of space waiting for anyone, anyone's voices to also be bounced down from the night sky. Are there other grievers out there? Dit dah. Stitch stitch. + Oh. I'd love to go into space. I think it would be really thrilling. Just to get in there and blast off. + Our longing made audible+ by our most romanticized celestial object, that great keeper of secrets—visible every night, even when seeming absent. Earth–Moon–Earth now a declassified radio relay technique allowing us to +ask the moon into our rooms.

+distorted
+read

Goodnight moon

I +

In Margaret Wise Brown's great green room there is a telephone and a red balloon and a picture of— and all the many named objects from a toyhouse to a mouse to a bowl full of mush for which the book will become known. Nearly everything in the great green room is twinned—the mittens, the kittens, the socks. And all the singular things are in complementary storybook pairs: a comb *and* a brush, the child *and* the old woman whispering *hush*. That *and* the miraculous language of turning one thing into two or more. Tethering each thing together, keeping them safe from floating off separately into the vastness of a child's dark room. Even the rising moon is neatly split in two—one half then the other divided by the gray line of a windowpane. To add + double + connect + join + gather + tell round and round + accumulate toward the gratifying click of an end rhyme that pins closed the story + room for the night.

> + —Chalk marks on the toile, or the V-shaped notches at the edges of the pattern pieces which indicate where they should join, mark the "future" of the dress. In this way, the pattern and the toile contain time within them, and a speculative future. +

The story actually goes: Brown began each day saying *Good morning* to every object in her room, settling her restless mind by listing what was. Good morning—. And good morning—. And—. Which could be to say: as children we have trouble getting into bed, worrying what will appear after the lights are turned out. Goodnight light and—. And when we are grown, we can't be sure we want to see what will reappear in the morning when the lights come up.

There is also a window split into panes and sets of twin asterisk stars tacked static in the night sky. And again and again in the great sometimes grayscale sky inside the book, there are a few white plus-sign +stars fastening the night sky to the nursery walls of each page, stitching together a panorama of the room.

+stitches +variants +chalk marks

+
Good morning moon
And good morning hospital room

| +

+ The moon reflects only part of the information back: some is absorbed in its shadows or lost in its craters. +

For months there's no reason for anyone to expect a second heartbeat to appear when the doctor eaves-drops into my body. No stray signals as the Doppler's soundwaves bounce around, reflecting off my moving blood cells. No previously known heredity. No reason to be dreaming double knots are gathering in the quiet dark, tied into a complex rig that keeps them from floating away in this endless salinity as they multiply into something that +might or +might not be. Here, the body's mimicry is not a metaphor—amniotic fluid is remarkably like the sea. Same salt, same proportion. And apparently just as shushing.

+will
+will

More months go by than most people believe is plausible to not know. They tell me it's like reality TV. These days could the doctors really? And me—could I—really? The unfathomableness of what I don't know can come undone:

+ a garment that can't be taken apart at the seams
+ too heavy to be dredged from the sea
+ a grief that will be suspended in the speculative future simple

Late into my second trimester, as a technician preps for a first ultrasound, as my sister distracts my fussing toddler by reading a book out loud, as the warbly black-and-white images surface on the screen, a gray line appears down the center like a seam—

+ Once there were twin color kittens with green eyes, Brush and Hush. +

I +

+ How many worlds can a garment inhabit at one time? + Let me reverse some of its stitches. In the city where I will be born an inventor will begin a humble company making latex bathing caps and swimwear. The company will grow larger, move cities, divide itself into different cells, some for the war effort and some for more +commercial manufacturing. After the war, women from surrounding towns will be hired to work on the lines at a newly announced division, Playtex, stitching bras and diaper covers and latex-dipping "living" girdles. Twenty-plus years into the future, it's seamstresses at Playtex who are initially tapped to move over to the handcrafting of spacesuits for the NASA astronauts.

+intimate

> + Because of the era's squeamishness about physicality, Dickinson and her contemporaries at times represented the body at one remove from the body: that is, through dress. +

Every other company's proposal for dressing + encasing the interstellar body in a military-engineered solution will fail. Their armor-like designs incapable of mimicking the human form or allowing a body to move with enough grace in low gravity. Hard-shell relics unsuited to carrying anyone to the moon. Playtex's flexible rubber girdle and the bra's nylon tricot was + is + will be the secret to fitting women's Earthly bodies into the restrictive garments of Dior's postwar "New Look" + the astronaut's bodies into spacesuits. A garment that holds both a future and a past body in its fabric. An impossible + otherworldly + fantastical body achievable only through an adept understanding of how to alter the figure underneath the architectural lines of the clothing. In other words, through the illusion + technology of undergarments.

Much of the language for the technical components and construction of the lunar spacesuits will be of the body: bladder, ribbed rings, webbing, joints. A language of intimacy and interiority. A language the seamstresses will already understand. Closer to earlier forms of *embodiment* in which we clothe a spirit with a body—a spacesuit: both an embodied body and an intervention of the body. The interior of the spacesuit touching the exterior of the body. The exterior touching endlessness+. Each latex-dipped component a well-guarded technique to a +fragile body dazzling us while bouncing through airlessness. Each of the spacesuit's seventeen concentric sheets of mylar glued by the seamstresses, thinner than single-thread lace. A body kept safe in the vastness of space through couture handiwork—a réseau of women rendering the moon possible with precision stitching and cutting and gluing. An abundance of hours.

+germlessness
+fleeting

1+

For many years traditional wedding dresses were made of dark, everyday fabrics—deep blues and browns and greens which could be worn more than once. After all, a worn-once dress is hardly economical when every garment is meticulously handstitched, seam and sleeve and pleat. An abundance of hours +embedded in every dress. The royal and well-off wore metallics or occasionally white. Not as in the future, to designate purity, but because the fabrics were expensive and so difficult to keep clean—a dazzling materialization of wealth that could be worn. An ordinary bride's dress was not often designed so much as designated—whatever your best dress happened to be was the one. On the rare occasion it was created new, afterward that dress + as is + altered + dyed was then bound to become your best. Worn until it was no longer.

+lost

A single nineteenth-century silk and lace wedding dress permanently tipped tradition from the necessity of rewearing dresses to a desire to use all those hours and hours of stitching for one-day splendor, and what would become the indelible Western tradition of lacy and virginal white. Though Queen Victoria's white was considered practical and patriotic, a color best suited to showing off the artisanal over the industrial. Her royal eighteen-foot train and abundant orange-blossom appliques, invitations for future fertility, were said to single-handedly revive Honiton lace-making. The otherwise relative understatement of her attire—her dress's simple silhouette, her wreath of already-fashionable wax flowers in lieu of a crown—set off a frenzy among brides-to-be who could now reasonably replicate + reproduce + repeat + twin her look. And they did, vanishing for over a century into the endless folds and lace.

+ —like any couture customer, the astronauts would often change their minds about fit details, sometimes causing their entire suit to be taken down to its components and carefully reassembled +

In my family, a white wedding dress is considered bad luck+. It's considered good luck if it rains at least a little on the day. Most marriages with a bride wearing white have drifted toward misfortune—or so my mother's and my aunts' stories go. A white dress is a dress in which no fault can be hidden+. To wear something in any other color is to attempt to hide the bride from the Fates—in their three stark white dresses with their glinting silver scissors ready to clamp + cut + clip even the shortest thread + smallest seam. In a white dress you might get lost in the light and lost again. In the closet, my mother's surviving + home-sewn + store-bought wedding dress, with its infamous red-wine stain buried so elegantly among multicolored polyester flowers it takes me years to find. Besides, it's hard to put grief into a white dress. Where in the fabric would it hide?

+an ill omen
+forgiven

> + So if you make a mistake—Like a needle hole—or something like that—Well if you don't admit that, that would be on your conscience all the time seems to me.+

I+

+stitched with a netlike weave that the
sea would respond to
+template +Xerox +knockoff +backup

Emily Dickinson's one white dress is a copy+. Of which there are actually two. Dickinson's one white plus twin replica dresses—make three. Three white dresses are not literary lore. They are the beginning of a bedtime story: *In the great green room there were three white dresses, three dresses in white that were*—acceptable to be worn around the house though not around town, sewn in a nineteenth-century style called a wrapper + housedress, meant for housework and harder wear and more often than not made of darker fabric. Though obviously not Dickinson's. Even if by then white cloth was considered easier to clean than fashionably bright aniline dyes and prints, might even have been considered more practical, her many white dresses still invited hot gossip. After all, other than brides + mourners, who only wears white? Dickinson's unlikely white dress is often speculated to be bridal, as if she considers herself wed to her poetry—or to God—or to herself. Dickinson's one white dress, in which she was always +talking to death.

+prepared for

But a historical artifact cannot be taken apart at the seams in order to make a pattern for twinning, cannot have its stitches +cut one by one. To make a new pattern from an existing garment that must remain intact is called "lifting" or "rubbing off." The dressmaker hired to twice replicate + lift Dickinson's one white dress had to imagine the pattern from seeing the dress already put together. Had to take it apart in her mind. Plan it backwards. The language of producing a facsimile dress is the language of the writer at work: *drafted—corrected—proofed—*. Only the first was likely a collective effort, drafted + patterned + stitched in a room with other women in intimacy.

+removed +undone +snipped

> + If it's possible to understand the ways in which people adapt to the unusual environment of zero gravity and sustained weightlessness, sustained long-duration space flight, then it's possible to understand really how people adapt to unusual environments on the Earth. +

It's difficult to know when entering the exhibit of her house which dress has been pulled out intact for display—the dress that embodied Dickinson's body + the dress that suggestively embodies her mind. The dress + the story we tell about her round and round. Hard to know in which she's hidden herself. In a white dress where would she hide? Three white dresses, each with fourteen yards of trim like the frill of a stamp's edge along the collar, the cuffs, the unexpected note-sized pocket with its envelope-flap closure. Only one with original embroidered lace. The iconic + dead-ringer dresses, one or the other, resting on a dress form in the east bedroom, arms bent as if about to take off. Her fair copy is kept safe in a glass case across town.

| +

+ As soon as the toile is completed it is taken apart. The separate parts serve as a pattern for the final garment. +

The iconic stork scissors used to cut + unpick intricate threads and stitches arrive to us in the future modified from midwives' clamps. The clamps were designed in the shape of the storks whose reappearance in the sky each spring marked the arrival of so many births—birds fabled to deliver babies to parents who had been good all winter. Stood upright on metal feet to keep them free of bacteria, the stork's long flat beak was rounded and offset, used to pinch closed umbilical cords + to clamp off rather than cut this shared thread of blood. Each time the midwives' clamps opened, a silver baby appeared swaddled in the body of the bird.

Or their long curved beaks were used to pick up cloth sterilized in boiling water before a birth. Or for pulling ribbons out of the tiny eyelet lace of new baby clothes before they were washed. Or, because it was considered an ill omen to announce a future birth directly in words, a pair would be placed carefully in a fireplace to reveal a baby was expected. A symbol of fertility +luck. Then, in case of complications or—, nothing would have to be +unsaid. The charred clamps could be buried discreetly somewhere away from the house.

+misfortune
+undone

Rumored in a pinch to also snip embroidery threads while the midwives whiled away the endless hours of someone else's labor, eventually the clamps were redesigned from a medical tool on hand in their kits into sharp-bladed scissors. First cast in silver and then, by the time I received my first pair, in gold, their pointed beaks easily slid between the stitches of +slippery wedding dress fabrics. To clamp + clip a dress off at its seams. As the storks were transformed into straight-handled scissors, they were often mistaken for cranes, and the silver baby in the body of the bird disappeared.

+fragile +dazzling

+ —the emotional poignancy attached to these garments is evidenced by their high survival rate in women's wardrobes +

Listen closely to any worn garment and you will find fine lines that mark details of construction + patterns of wear + indications of more than one wearer. Signs of possible variation + annotation + distortion—initials embroidered along a pocket + the strain in a buttonhole that might indicate a garment was worn during early stages of pregnancy + the ellipsis of holes showing stitching has been undone—seams and hems let down + let out + in. These lines will allow you to draw the garment + take it apart in your mind + translate its cut and composition onto the page. Create an image + a pattern if the garment is read aloud + help calculate the relationship of one part + one wearer of a garment to another. +

Listen. I am reading the garment out loud.

I +

In the town where I was born there is a collective of women deconstructing donated wedding dresses. Unrooting pleats and sleeves and hems one by one by hand in their spare time. One by one by one the silhouette of each gown undone and repatterned into burial garments+ for babies who die in Labor and Delivery or in the Neonatal ICU.

+—an endless garment, one that is woven of everything—for this garment without end is proffered through a text which is itself unending.

Goodnight light and—

Listen closely and you'll overhear, stitched inside the lines and repetitions and rhymes of Margaret Wise Brown's *Goodnight Moon*, the modernist, staccato repetitions of Gertrude Stein. It shouldn't have been surprising to discover Stein was Brown's favorite author. Or to learn it was Brown who first suggested Stein might write a splendid children's book. How obvious now to imagine the possibilities of Stein's playfulness reaching the ears of young children, their curiosity reflecting off all that dazzling language—as if her words had been found bouncing along the surface of the moon. As if Stein's future rose-colored children's book, *The World Is Round*, was first transmitted out into space.

Eight years into the future, Margaret Wise Brown's *Goodnight Moon* will deconstruct Gertrude Stein's lavish modernist line, retranscribe it into lullaby, alter its syntactical fabric by letting each individual sound sing, rather than be saturated by proximity to so many other Steinian repetitions and syllables. As if *Goodnight Moon*, with all those absences and pauses and repetitions, is what Brown heard retransmitted back to her here on Earth. Among the bowl and brush, the little bears and their chairs, the clocks and the socks, the light to which we say goodnight, and the floating red balloon, the moon is here in the room. Restitched + undone into a child's wild and simple declarations—Brown's uncanny ability to capture children's worlds using a child's perspective of words. A here and now that makes a story go round and round.

+ Sudden say separate.
So great so great Emily.
Sew grate sew grate Emily. +

Stein chose the same artist to illustrate *The World Is Round* as the one who would go on to paint Brown's iconic great green room in *Goodnight Moon*.

A room that has been criticized by countless parents for looking like no one's childhood bedroom ever. That color palette! The scale! Though this is apparently untrue. The great green room was inspired by details of Brown's own childhood. The framed nursery rhymes hanging on its walls recalled illustrated tiles around the fireplace in her and her sister's bedroom. Brown's use of repetition and variation as you flip each page contains the physical memory of the feeling of being in a childhood space. As if the story were a room + garment you could step into, recross the twilight line of time, overhear it again as it was last read out loud. Each spare pair of red, often-rhyming lines are tucked into the corners, anchoring the edges of the room. Each of the eight panoramas of the room with less and less light on the paper as the illustrated moon rises across the window, as we read toward a final goodnight addressed out into an everywhere. The black letters stitched under the alternating grayscale images keeping us from drifting off into the nothingness of the white sky of these nearly blank pages.

+ Are you – Nobody – too?
Then there's a pair of us! +

I +

At any given time just one of Emily Dickinson's white dresses is planted in her bedroom like a flag on the moon, + stiff and awkward, trying to float on a breeze that does not blow. + A room that has been celebrated for housing a mind that looked like no one else's mind ever. And this is apparently true, for – put them side by side –+. A mind capable of making poems like lace, full of gaps and pauses and absences. All those variants letting us listen in as she works out a live problem on the page. All those em-dashes with dots over the top, turning connective pauses into birds, inviting us to leap from one space to the next. To keep the vast horizon of her mind in line. As if her words were signals bounced from places more vast than we can imagine—reflected off the moon's surface—returned to us overheard.

+– hold them – Blue to Blue –

I +

When the astronauts bounce back down from the moon, they are immediately isolated due to a fear of microbes and germs, of a moon plague coming back with the crew to Earth to infect us all. They fear something out of a comic book has gathered itself in the quiet dark of outer space—multiplying into something that might or might not be. An unknown that could undo us all. For eighty-eight hours after hurtling back to Earth the astronauts survive inside a space-age Isolette unit—a hopped-up Silver Bullet trailer known as "the mobile quarantine unit." They press their faces to the rear window for interviews and gimmicky photo ops while the nation peers in at the spectacle of them in their blue flight suits.

> + It was getting darker and darker and there was no moon, Rose never cared about the moon but there were lots of stars—

They would spend another three weeks in a larger quarantine area undergoing test after test before being let back out into the world. It didn't seem to matter that NASA scientists knew the intense unlikelihood of lunar life. Or that the rest of us Earthlings may have already been exposed when the astronauts' capsule was opened to retrieve them—infectiousness instantly airborne, blown out over the ocean.

> —and somebody had told her that stars were round, they were not stars—and so the stars were not any comfort to her and just then well just then—*Just then* wailed Rose *I wish just then had been a hen.* +

| +

To the parents who had not been good all winter—or who had not taught their children to be—to those parents, the mother instructed her young storks each spring to deliver a baby that had dreamed itself to death in the lake where babies wait before being born. Or so the nineteenth-century story was told as a +warning, round and round.

+punishment

I +

> + And as they slept they dreamed their dream—A wonderful dream of a red rose tree that turned all white when you counted three.
> One . . . Two . . . Three +

I will leave the doctor with a sequence of grainy pictures that look like they were taken on the +sea-floor, forms labeled A and B with arrows that say: *girl parts*. I will not have a chance to register the evidence of this twinning existence before there are complications. I will return to my doctor because I am dizzy. There will be shadows on the scan. When I look closely, misplaced things. As the maker of this future possible I will feel responsible somehow for this misplacement. I will tell myself it's not because I wasn't immediately excited about multiplying something else in the quiet dark. At first, I was scared.

+moon

I will find out what *complication* might mean alone in a hotel room minutes before being picked up for a day-long job interview. I will take a nude self-portrait of my still-doubling body in the hotel mirror. I will understand this as evidence for myself. I will gather myself into my blackest suiting dress as if in future mourning. I will keep it in my closet for years longer than necessary. I will never rewear it. I will be told to prepare for a decision. I will be told round and round total loss is not the worst-case scenario. I will be offered the job. I will understand this as—. I will not be able to imagine a future, any future, in order to take it + to make it. Later I will live in that future.

For future safety, the medical record of all this will be stricken + bounced back with dots and dashes of the code missing. For my own good, what's +done will be +done. Each time I revisit this moment I will cross the gray line that splits the Goodnight Moon in two, stepping from one side to the other.

What's left+ will exist only as documentary photographs displayed in sequential order. Depending on which direction you read them—two living future possibles + one future undoing itself. To keep them from floating to the surface I will ask they be +hidden somewhere in the house.

+gone
+gone
+undone
+undone

+Nothing will be left to accumulate salt.
+I will be left as evidence.

+buried

And then there was +Rosa.

+Rosa was her name and would she have been +Rosa if her name had not been +Rosa. We used to think and then we used to think again.

Would she have been +Rosa if her name had not been +Rosa and would she have been +Rosa if she had not been a twin.

+Rosa was her name all the same—

<table>
<tr><td>+Twin A</td><td></td></tr>
<tr><td>+Twin B</td><td></td></tr>
<tr><td>+Twin A</td><td>+Twin B</td></tr>
<tr><td>+Twin A</td><td></td></tr>
<tr><td>+Twin B</td><td>+Twin A</td></tr>
<tr><td>+Twin B</td><td></td></tr>
<tr><td></td><td></td></tr>
<tr><td>+Rose</td><td></td></tr>
<tr><td></td><td></td></tr>
<tr><td>+Rose</td><td></td></tr>
<tr><td>+Rose</td><td></td></tr>
<tr><td></td><td>+Rose</td></tr>
</table>

I +

> + – altered a little – will be my only one +

For over a century there has been just one verifiable photograph of Dickinson. In the iconic black-and-white + silver daguerreotype, she is not wearing the white dress. She's a teenager fixed in a dress she will live in forever. And that dress is made in an undefinable, dark printed fabric with a slight sheen. Not surprising, given dark fabrics were considered more suitable as they kept sitters from becoming spectral blurs—there and not there. But people will mostly forget this first dress. There's nothing spectacular + singular about it. The daguerreotype era produces millions of replica dark dresses. There's no narrative we can attach to its +common folds. The white fabric arrives in the future.

+cotton

One hundred years of one documentary photograph and one surviving white dress going round and round, depicting Dickinson as an ethereal-looking teenager superimposed over an ethereally dressed adult. Even as it's been told round and round that nobody at the time considered the image a particularly good likeness. Until a second possible daguerreotype is uncovered. In the image there are two women, two dresses. One dress a griever's black speculated to be worn by a recently widowed friend. The other, when magnified, revealed to be checks—a grid of fine lines woven through the fabric. A pattern that was considered best for daguerreotypes, a perfect contrast in the folds between light and dark. Like the original, the portrait is so small it requires intense forensic attention+ to gather information about the possible wearers and their dresses.

+obsession

The Emily Dickinson Museum textile collection is searched. A possible copy of the pattern and sheen of this second daguerreotype dress is found. Fabric with light-gray and white threads creating a réseau on a stunning blue background. Swatches of a +blue dress that were saved + deconstructed + stitched onto paper backing to be reused, along with other snips of bright dress silks and plaid satins, as part of a hexagon quilt block. A match that might verify Dickinson is the wearer and begin to unfasten the afterimage of a monochromatic era of Victorian mourning wear.

+future possible +already made

Difficult to then undo the collective image of Dickinson the artist in her singular + sonogramic white dress. What would we do with her + would we recognize her if she came to us in blue? This new future-possible Dickinson would be a Dickinson in process + in sequence—stitching and unstitching—patterning her poems and not yet on the moon. A variant + twin Dickinson who changes ages, changes dresses between acts from dark to blue to white—who might allow for distortion, for distance between the first dress and the last and now. A panoramic view of her materiality that pins herself to herself. In the absence of a physical dress, we have to reimagine her in a blue wider than the sky, in the long seconds she was suspended + exposed—there and not there—sitting impossibly still as the camera's lens remained open, arm around a mourning friend, before the salt fixes + gathers her back into black-and-white like moonlight on the daguerreotype's silver surface.

I +

+ ACT I. Count her dresses. ACT II. Collect her dresses. ACT III. Clean her dresses. +
+ ACT III. Can you draw a dress. +

It can take years to pattern + put together + perfect a new magic trick before it can be performed without indecorously showing its seams. We don't often get to watch how these garments come together + apart. Here is the toile of a trick I once overheard: In 1983, a famous magician gathers other magicians in a dark parking lot to watch him practice for his spectacular plan to vanish the Statue of Liberty in front of a live audience. To rehearse out any possible knots in his performance, he first attempts to disappear something more common and accessible to us all: the full moon from the night sky. Afterward, like any magician worth his salt, he will ask for notes to help fine-tune the illusion.

A clear late-winter evening, the sun blown out early enough for everyone to stay alert. The stage monumental. The mechanism, with any luck, so imperceptible as to go unnoticed even by a collective of experts. You know what they say—if you can fool a stitch of magicians into believing you've disappeared+ the moon and all its dust from the night sky—the moon there and not there—you can fool anyone. Or so the story goes.

+pulled

It appears this moon rehearsal was successful, because early that spring—as helicopters buzzed in the starlessness around her iconic crowned head—as even farther above her the first *Challenger* prepared to reenter orbit after its maiden flight—the magician raised an enormous diaphanous fabric, mesmerizing both a live and home audience into believing the lady behind it would vanish right before their eyes.

Thirty-two years later to the day, and eleven weeks too early, doctors and residents and nurses are gathering in Labor and Delivery to disappear a future possible from a cut seam.

And she does. The stage turns. The fabric falls. The audience is looking out at the nothingness of a night+ sky hovering above empty water. The first tracking and data relay satellite now recording stray signals, listening invisibly overhead. Every stiff fold of her ninety-four-foot patinaed green dress, gone.

+unveiled +veiled

| +

The tradition of matching bridesmaids and attendants begins with a bride hiding in her own dress, disappearing herself in front of a live audience, keeping herself hard to find until the knot is tied and the ceremony is over. A knot of women gathering round and round her in replica dresses—making it unclear who is in the real wedding dress and who is wearing a variant—in order to confuse +dybbuks and keep them from +entering the bride's soul. The trick is turning one bride + one dress into many.

+the Fates
+cutting the finishing knot

> + In the final stages—the multilayered, human-shaped assembly could not be folded or squashed under a normal sewing machine, and instead had to be sewed on two Singer machines modified—so an entire suit could be moved under its needle. +

If dresses are accumulating + appearing + disappearing like steadily multiplying cells+, how does one document the existence of the variants? The artist's collaborator straps 150 pounds to his body to stay still on the seafloor, photographing and filming the black gown as crystals gather across its surface—every thread and pleat replicating slowly in salt. The resulting footage sounds like a Foley artist's idea of water moving over something. Of someone trying not to breathe in a liquid space. A sonic negative image of the dress like an ultrasound on loop.

+brides

After the full-size dress could not be lifted out whole, a scaled-down version, a bridesmaid, was produced under the same conditions. *Small Salt Bride*—a dress+

successfully removed from the water intact for display. The two sculptures are quite often conflated, but the full-length Rovina replica exists only as documentary photographs—eight dresses displayed in sequential order like phases of the moon, in heavier and heavier stages of salt and then of light on film. On the surface it's a similar sleight of hand to the one Queen Victoria performed: turning an iconically dark dress to a megawatt white. A color signaling the beginning + end of mourning.

+a daughter

In the final photograph, a fully crystallized bride materializes in the depths. The first seven dresses are in process, waxing or waning depending on which way you enter the exhibit. An empty dress and an empty dress again and again as it twins or untwins itself.

I +

+ Then Space – began to toll,
As all the Heavens were a Bell, +

According to ceremony, prior to a funeral service mourners are required to rend their garments, exposing their hearts by tearing a worn piece of clothing. The rending must take place during the time of most intense grief, not after + later. The grieving must be recent. The tearing must be done at once. The tearing should be done as a collective effort. Every heart exposed in sequence—a creak across the soul—the mourners to and fro. The garments then discarded—the soul let—

As it is a time of +inviolate joy, even in grief, during the first seven days after a +marriage, +brides must not take part in the tearing. They must request someone else's garment be rendered undone on their behalf. Even in inviolate grief, their wedding dresses must remain +complete.

+unalterable +birth +mothers +unaltered

In the absence of a gathering + fabric + a funeral. Without a ritual of rending, of a tearing at the heart-of, of an exposing what cannot be undone. In the midst of this treading—treading—might mothers who have recently—wrecked, solitary, here—ask others to do this undoing for us. To pull as many one white dresses down as stray signals of grief.

The sanctioned destruction of dress meant to offer relief: *keriah*—the sound of fabric being split somewhere other than a seam. Like a cry.

In the great gray room—There was no telephone—And no red balloons—And no picture of—And there were no flowers sitting on chairs—Or congratulatory cards for pairs—No sets of socks for the tiny arrivals—And no comb and no brush—No quiet old grandmother whispering hush. There was nothing shining. In the great gray room—There was—A pair of hospital beds—And a recovering new mother—And a resident repeatedly requesting a signature for burying the dead.

Goodnight stars   Goodnight air

+

+

| +

+ The dress may not even be made in the house where she lives. It must be sewn elsewhere, and during the sewing a needle must not be broken. The fabric for a wedding dress may not be ripped, it must be cut with scissors. +

When one twin dies in utero + at birth and the other survives, they are known alternately as *sunset sunrise* twins. If you listen closely in the hours between night and day, day and night, at sunrise + sunset, you'll hear stray signals as they multiply. Voices overheard through an open window. A cry accidentally picked up on the same channel as someone else's baby monitor. This thin seam that separates daylight and darkness and daylight—here and not here—is known as the gray line + terminator + twilight zone. Shortwave radio operators watch this line move slowly across the Earth in order to know when they might reach people they might not otherwise be able to. During the day there's too much radiation in the lower layers of the ionosphere and it muffles the signal. At night there aren't enough ions to return signals intact. At both times signals attempted to be sent across greater distances can become frayed or disappear. In the gray line what is sent out bounces back faster + clearer + farther with less degradation or distortion. Earth–Moon–Earth radio transmission is not affected by the gray line but requires specialized antennas, precision and skill, to be able to chart the moon as it moves across the sky. Most of us wouldn't know about it, or how to do it, unless we had a need to know. What's left for those of us who are trying to listen is this gray line between the living hours of the day and the dead hours of the night. When we imagine what's lost might still return to us on Earth.

Listen, we are entering the gray line—

> \+ For perhaps as much as five minutes,
> the astronauts were alive and conscious
> and yet knew that death was certain. +

I +

It is suggested you consider wearing white—that you avoid wearing leather shoes or belts—that you write down a particular failure as you enter the room—that you are ready to seek + ask forgiveness—have already sought it—that you are ready to be forgiven. This is a tradition in which we +rehearse. Break all vows. Annul our previous year. We dress as in a burial +shroud. We dress to be ready for death + life. We are wrapped in white as when we are wed—as when we are buried—as after we are born. In all white we are anonymous and together as one. On the threshold of the living and the—waiting—waiting—to know in which of the twin +books we will be written in the coming year. A white dress is a dress ready for death.

+prepare +gown +dresses

Let us begin this Kol Nidre remembering a sermon given thirty years before—during another Yom Kippur, in the year of the *Challenger* coming undone. It had just come to light that the seven astronauts did not likely die immediately. The rabbi of then + the rabbi of this future asks each of us gathered in the room to imagine how the astronauts may have been preparing. How might the living practice for our own inevitable disappearance from the night sky. Again and again. How might we address the many future-possible *If only I had*—. Can we amend how we live now so we will be ready. Less regretful in the last minutes before our capsule hits the water. Before we are lost in the light and lost again. Adrift in our whitest garments in airlessness.

Three Yom Kippurs after he gives the initial sermon the rabbi will die alongside his wife and many others when their plane goes down. A forty-minute crash landing for which he might have been more uniquely prepared than most. His children somehow, miraculously, survive and describe the reassurance he offered as they hurtled out of the sky—

> + Can you imagine knowing that in a few moments death was imminent? —If, God forbid, you and I were in such circumstances? —What would go through our mind? What went through their minds. —I want you to consider on this Yom Kippur, what If? What if I had five minutes to live? +

I +

After you register your name and the time, you head to a containment room where you have to scrub in before you are allowed to enter the sterile Isolettes area. There are signs everywhere explaining the simple instructions: wash continuously up to your elbows with soap for a full three minutes. Skip this step and you could contaminate others. In a system this precarious any contamination could lead to death.

After scrubbing yourself + totally clean, germless, without bacteria, like the surface of the moon, + you will walk through the automatic sliding doors—your arms raised—bent at the elbows as if about to take off—palms facing your face—the way every surgeon in every TV show you have ever seen walks into an operating room. You must not touch anything + anyone on the way through.

> + Are there signs—for example, small pinholes or stitch marks—that any decoration has been removed +

After we walked our stitchwork out onto the moon, how long did it take before we had a better understanding of the likely bacterialessness of space? Every so often there are reports of new species of bacteria found on the International Space Station, ones that were undocumented before launch. Reports that point to what might survive in space or how we might contaminate each other and other planets when we attempt to travel beyond the moon. Likely these are resilient Earth microorganisms, accidental contamination hitching a ride in the fold of a seam. We are after all formed from a wild collision. How can we expect to tell the dust of ourselves from ourselves.

I +

> + There is something mysterious, too, in the possibility that the gaps in the music might represent a sort of sonic negative image of the moon's topography, with each missing note indicating some lunar crater or gulf in which the original signal was lost. +

Down the hall from the birthing ward through the automatic doors, inside an Isolette unit as germless as the surface of the moon, a sunrise + surviving + twin + untwinned daughter is bathed in unearthly blue light to break down her dangerous bilirubin. Good morning hospital room. The first three days she is alive her face is hidden beneath a mask protecting her retinas, making her look like a small blue hen. This is a detail that is only charming in a future retelling, one of those unexpected details + stitches that allow a story to go round and round. How humor makes grief bearable, reveals a garment's history, lets us alter the narrative to make a different pattern. I don't want to admit I have trouble visiting for the first week.

Good morning light and—

The next few weeks of her life she survives in an incubator adapted from one that first appeared in a sideshow at Coney Island's Luna Park, where a doctor received preterm babies from parents after hospitals presumed them lost causes. These babies were so tiny they were considered attractions, too expensive and too risky to allow people to hope they might be kept alive + survive. Those who needed to know, or who had heard of those who needed to know, shared word of how admission costs were used to hire round-the-clock nurses. Each day thousands of people entered the exhibit, paying to press their faces to the spectacle behind the incubators' glass, to peer in at the infinitesimal preemies—little chicks wrinkled up in their warm quarantines.

Good morning noises everywhere—

1+

According to ritual the naming of a baby should take place in the first eight days + the naming should take place thirty days after a birth has occurred + the naming should be done at once. A baby should + should not be named after the living + the dead. When the first baby is born, she is named after my mother. And after she is born, it is agreed in a future future, when + if there is a second child her name will come from another beloved relative. Her name will be Rosa. Rosa will be her name her name.

Rosa was her name and for days we called her Unofficially Rosa—and the nurses all called her Unofficially Rosa—and why couldn't we make it official? they said. When does Unofficially Rosa become officially a Rosa and when does a Rosa become unofficially a twin. Would Rosa be her name all the same? I tell you at this time the world was all round and you could go on it round and around.

On the second night going round and round my hospital room unable to sign a name + the certificate, when a nurse tells me she's chosen *Unofficially Rosa* to look out for—her little moon clementine—despite all the bruising the wires the chicken mask over her eyes—no word for the relief of someone else finally celebrating her tiny +arrival. Someone else going round and round, listing her as something that exists in the room before the lights are turned out and again in the morning when they come back up.

+survival

If one twin was a Rosa the other twin had been not
a Rosa and then I had chosen which of the twins
had died. We all had names and her name was Rosa—
but would she have been, I used to cry about it, would
she have been Rosa if her name had not been Rosa.
Would she have been Rosa if she had not been a twin.
Rosa was her name all the same.

| +

\+ A wedding dress is not a NASA spacesuit. This is not a highly technical item of apparel. You know how to do this. You may think you don't, but you know how. You have bought clothes. You've dressed yourself for years. +

The endless garment of hospital time: more than once I overhear a family in the crowded elevator complaining they have been coming so many days in a row they have trouble remembering where they parked their car. How many days have they been here? —Less than a week. I don't tell them I'm on week seven, day forty-eight—week eight, day fifty-six—week nine—. I suggest they take a photo when they park. I don't tell them this trick took me longer to put together than I care to admit. That actually, I overheard it. That I often wandered the concentric circles of the parking garage bereft for an hour or more as the sun went down, trying to relocate myself, losing more and more time to be back down on the ground with my other child. Clicking my keys again and again in hopes my car would blink itself back into existence. I quietly seethe at the people who fail to be careful, but the ones who really undo me are those carrying infant car seats, marking them as people as I once was, in a variant life—whose baby + babies arrived safely + are about to return to Earth.

For all but one bath during the first two months of her life, she is tied into a complex rig of tubes and lines that means I have to watch out for possible knots. I will not be allowed to carry her more than a couple feet away from a bassinet, even once she is moved to a regular room. Every new parent understands the necessity of rocking, walking, swaying with a newborn. All those fussing, sleepless hours spent consoling without the grace of +motion. Another immeasurable loss. And the endless dit + dah +

dit + dah of her monitors, sounds I will keep dreaming + overhearing for years after I leave for the last time. The NICU, it turns out, is one of the loudest places on Earth. When+ babies go home they often have trouble sleeping without noises everywhere.

+gravity

+If

| +

+ They were so excited to have become astronauts, and then to actually be to the point of putting on the suit they'd wear in space. It was almost like a bride-to-be getting fitted for her wedding gown. +

The longer we are in quarantine the deeper the resentment for visitors who fail to scrub in correctly or long enough, who might pose a life-or-death risk because they are lazy. Because their baby is mostly fine and doesn't need to fear bacteria or a failure to fight off some common microbe. And isn't forgetting every few hours how to breathe. Possibly one of those horrible families whose baby was born on time but just has some small issue so they are in the NICU for monitoring, who won't spend enough time here to accumulate salt. Those babies are species from another planet. Those families are watching the rest of us on the moon from afar. As a televised scene. We, on the other hand, are +stranded. Are not bouncing back down. At home, my other child—the one named Sallie, after my mother—is too young, too germy, to be allowed to join us. For ten weeks she doesn't even meet this new sibling. What is a Rosa who is there and not there? My aunt gifts her a baby doll to help prepare for our eventual reentry. She names it Fake Baby Rosa and carries it everywhere.

+lost in the craters

On the moon there is no foreseeable future. An endless here and now and now of a children's storybook. Everyone not on the moon with the two of us is scared of the baby or for her + thinks we are or could be the plague. No one wants to be contaminated by +future-possible loss. My own family is mostly incapable of visiting the two of us up here, their grief keeping them from returning to the site of a still-recent loss. So anxious about causing another. About being the cause of—. And I get it. Labor and Delivery, the NICU, and the ICU my mother died in are all threaded together by the same elevator. I cross and recross the gray line of hospital time. I live again and again in my own ability to be a maker of +death.

+grief +grief

Waking each day before dawn to call and ask a nurse if the note about being fed slowly has been lost again in the shuffle, preparing to hear the baby is back in a high-risk area + needs another spinal tap + blood draw + scan to try to understand what new infection has blown out over her body. For decades longer than you'd believe was possible—until far after we saw the Earth from the perspective of the moon—doctors believed babies couldn't feel pain and operated on them without anesthetic. Even now, knowing this is false, it wouldn't be safe to sedate such a tiny body for every possible complication. Many diagnostic procedures are aided only by the sweet-taste analgesic of sugar water on a finger. The moon, it turns out, is the opposite of the amniotic sea—all those sugar crystals accumulating on babies' tongues, keeping them safe from drifting+ off into space.

+dreaming at the bottom of the lake

| +

+ The moon, on the other hand, is a poor place for flags—What a pity that in our moment of triumph—we did not plant instead a device acceptable to all: a limp white handkerchief, perhaps, symbol of the common cold— +

Fifty years after the moon landing, when the world finds itself in a large-scale quarantine, people will struggle with washing their hands for only twenty continuous seconds. They will have to create apps to turn a favorite song into a twenty-second hand-washing rendition to sing when returning from the infected outside world. I will be uniquely prepared for the isolation and constant fear of germs and contagion.

In the before-pandemic world when I start writing this, it will be impossible to describe to others the relentless anxiety of the NICU, that everything everything is a possible contagion, and on any given day any of us are capable of being carriers of someone else's death. Our bodies are not the moon. How a usually harmless germ from my toddler might have tucked itself inside my nose or inside the fabric of my clothes. Or yours. We are not the moon. Though it was + is total +isolation. The unbearable confusion of leaving a baby to be tended by others night after night after night. To not know which place to be, with one child or the other. Or the other. In some elsewhere I didn't + don't have time to imagine. Let alone what would happen if I put on my blackest dress and traveled toward her instead.

+annihilation

Day 1—Day 2—Day 3—Day 4—. I know to stop around Day 12—. It's easier when you lose track of the number of stitches to be +surprised when a garment finally comes + apart + together. In this future version of the world, I will be relieved that we are in a shared containment space. My children's germs and my own will be capable of infecting each other equally. Whatever Earth plague has been blown from over the ocean will likely come for each of us, together, waiting in our warm quarantine. We resent everyone. No one in particular will be to blame.

+relieved

| +

\+ And a lot of times we're sewing or making things and maybe the girl next to you is doing the same thing but we never see the suit put together. +

Sometimes sections of the donated dresses are requested by the bestower to be saved so they can be worn in a speculative future, pulled from an attic as something old + borrowed + blue. An heirloom. Then the women undoing the dresses will carefully assess your gown. Suggest ways you might +rescue parts of it for your +daughter. For years, more dresses will be offered up to the seamstresses than are necessary. An affluence of dresses. A fever of dresses. An empty dress and an empty dress and an empty dress like steadily accumulating +cells. Each wedding dress dividing + multiplying as if in future mourning. Again and again undone. To be +worn just once, this one white—.

+restore +remove
+soon-to-be +not-to-be
+salt
+buried +donated

By the time I hear about them, the seamstresses are no longer looking for any dresses to be pulled down from the quiet dark of someone's closet. With the exception of dresses coming from mothers who have *recently*—. For whom the donation may be a way of surviving or beginning to grieve. Who might otherwise not bury their dresses. The women never specify what amount of time *recently* might mean.

These women in intimacy in a living room undoing, their slow unsewing. Their work a careful tearing open of a sewn piece of clothing. In the past + future, I will spend an inordinate amount of time staring into a photograph of this room in the newspaper from my hometown. Trying to glean something about these seamstresses who gather to undo, to make garments for future possibles still multiplying + dividing in the quiet dark. I'm trying to understand if I would be allowed+ to join this collective. To take these garments apart. To remove any record of a previous wearer. To be allowed to rend how undone you've become with grief. To make it public, to make it quick. To make it private, measured. To undo just once this one white dress. To have unsaid *I do*. To be the undoer. To be allowed to be undone. Done.

+want

If a death isn't recent, you cannot donate your dress. + If your dress isn't white, you cannot donate it. + If a death isn't recent, you cannot tear it + wear it. If a death isn't recent, you can't undo + bury it. What then is left for these unbearable +grievers?

+mothers

|+

+ This is how we walk on the moon—
This is how we walk on the moon—
This is how we walk on the moon +

Twenty-four years before Queen Victoria's notorious white dress—a dress that was actually not white so much as cream or even light pink, that was not in fact the first white dress worn by royalty, that was only rendered stark white in artistic depictions of the wedding sent around the world as souvenirs—the beloved Princess Charlotte wore an elaborate empire-waisted wedding dress made entirely in metallic silver. Silver lamé on silk net over a silver tissue slip. Hard to imagine such a sheer, space-age dress in the early nineteenth century—a dress with lace made of threads of actual metal, woven of a color that in the future we will associate with dreaming up the future and all that's to come. The same color as the dress her mother had worn. A silver dress absolutely meant to dazzle an audience while she stood in the unfiltered light, in which otherworldliness might have suddenly seemed nearer+.

+nearer than the sky—

Charlotte and her dress: the reflection of a full moon—the last of the silver gowns before Victoria disappears both bright and dark dresses inside the folds of so much white lace and white satin fabric. Though even Victoria understood the importance of thrift and reuse of splendor—repurposing her veil and the lace of her dress again and again for other garments across the years. Even after she turns her one white dress to deep black in mourning.

For many years, white was actually considered the traditional choice for mourning. A color easily achieved by sun-bleaching fabric. Only a white dress a dress ready for death. As black dye was expensive and required multiple rounds of dyeing to achieve a deep hue, true black as the pervasive shade of grief didn't arrive until the synthetic dyes of the future. It appeared first as a dazzling materialization of wealth that only the royal bereaved could wear. The first royal to wed in white, in 1558, actually caused quite a stir. Did she arrive to mourn or to marry?

Charlotte and her dress reflecting off the glint of the Fates' sharp scissors. One year after her wedding she will die of complications after giving birth to a stillborn son—a trick of turning what was once two into none. Her dress pulled +silver from the night sky will be kept as an heirloom in the quiet dark of a future archive—so frail now the fine silk net and its pattern of silver dashes disintegrates at the slightest touch. Charlotte's one unwhite dress that doesn't save her—that will never be allowed to +be taken apart at the seams.

+intact
+show its decorous seams

+ To maintain a quiet environment for healing and growing and to protect privacy, please avoid talking or lingering in the hallways. +

I +

So many needle holes and needles + errant pins left in Dickinson's poems. Not all for sewing. Some used to wound + puncture + stab + mark. And the way she chose to stitch her poems—leaving audible pinholes in their fabric—morse code notes poked straight through the pages—that allow us in the future to take all those undone white sheets, restitch + unstitch them back together in sequence. A panorama of poems + a mind in the gray line between daylight and darkness. Undo each poem + dress and what's left are the ellipsis of pinholes—dots and dashes—traveling across the fabric + page.

The dressmaker hired to multiply Dickinson's one white dress first would have made a toile, a practice

+ draft dress made in muslin, meant to be taken apart to turn into a pattern that could be twinned and twinned and twinned, turning one dress into many. Meaning there are or were likely four possible dresses: the original, the two replicas, and the toile that would have been undone—a speculative future dress + ghost of the final dresses returned to its prestitched state. A toile is a garment made to be altered, to never be worn. Each of these duplicate heirlooms that will never contain Dickinson's or anyone's future body. Or her reason for adopting such dazzling fabric for workwear. Dickinson's multiplying variants + dresses + pinholes, turning her into many, keeping mourners from creaking across her soul. Dickinson, who was + constantly more astonished that the Body contains the Spirit + or that clothes could then contain the body at all.

> + Originally conservators used flashlights to peer inside the neck or wrist openings, but that process revealed little about how the suits were actually built—But short of taking them apart we really couldn't tell what was going on inside. +

What a pity that instead of a flag we did not plant a copy of Dickinson's paper-white dress on the moon—symbol of the common poem— + which, like the moon, affects us all, unites us all. + Each month going round and round—turning from light to dark to the moon's silver glint and back again depending on whether it's waxing or waning. As if underneath her one luminous white dress is its exact space-black lace replica waiting to hurtle back to Earth.

|+

+ Every change to the suit—including both changes in dimension to suit each astronaut, and changes in configuration to enhance individual astronauts' comfort—called for enormous additional documentation—this was tantamount to arguing that a shirt or pair of trousers became a different object when altered, or even buttoned— +

When I marry I hedge my bets and wear a blue silk dress. So trite it's true: something old + something new + something borrowed + something blue. A dress that is not a wedding dress to begin with and requires a seamstress to painstakingly unstitch section after section to add a bustle to the train, so I don't step on the hems and rip the dress at the seams while wearing it. Its dark fabric is a near match to an archived fragment I find of a dress worn for a wedding in 1727—a blue likely chosen to be worn again and again. My blue is less practical, the head-to-toe concentric layers of raw-edged satin + silk sewn carefully into a mesh net like the thin photographic slices of the moon stitched together to map its surface. No single layer is wider than a finger. It +cannot possibly +be undone into something else. I am many garments and more moons away from becoming a mother who has recently—. Who could possibly know burial garments are often made from white wedding dresses stripped back to their nearly prestitched state. Only a white dress a dress ready for death. In every future house: two unwhite unready wedding dresses. My mother's and mine.

+will not
+be light on the moon

In the future one daughter will apologize that she only wants the blue dress to wear to a party, will claim if she ever chooses to marry, she'll wear a silver jumpsuit with silver sneakers. Something simple and sparkly, like a bow, on her head. I don't blame her. She'll be the moon. And in a future future, after this grief undoes me + my marriage + my wife—seam by seam—until we cannot make it fit—after all what is a marriage that is both there and not there—I will watch the way silver lamé moves like liquid metal and be inclined to consider it for my future myself. A moon of moons. Though I imagine I will actually marry again in the folds of carefully sewn seams, amid the gorgeous orange-and-green polyester flowers my mother picked out, repatterning my way back through the dots and dashes of initial stitchwork—altering the signals and lines until the dress turns from hers into mine.

But in this future, I can't bring myself to undo it. To undo + rewear + ready a surviving dress means to disappear the evidence of the story of the wine stain, the dirt all over the hems, the record of her measurements, how I was told it was made by her mother but find a tag partially cut off in an altered seam, to give up another part of her that is already both here and not here. Instead, I find a vintage orange dress whose previous maker + wearer is unknown. As if my mother's dress had been transmitted out into space and this is what had bounced back down from the moon—dit dah, stitch stitch. Hanging together in my closet, twin polyester dresses. Only one +that fits like it was made for me.

In another future, I will recognize that three dresses can only become the opening of a story when you are looking back from the future, gathering the dots and dashes. A dress is a dress ready for death. To begin again is to be+ inside another garment entirely.

+I don't have to alter
+I will begin again

| +

+ —Dresses do not need to be in perfect
condition—can have stains or tears. +

So little evidence of the seamstresses' process or day-to-day work exists, other than the empty spacesuits themselves. Some now so fragile they're disintegrating from the inside out. Not the seamstresses' +card-stock patterns used to trace and cut each piece, not the scans of these patterns recording the changing lines of the suit. Only the engineering blueprints, from which the seamstresses learned to construct these patterns, were considered ephemera important enough to keep. Or the réseau marks on the moon-landing photographs, superimposing each spacesuit with barely visible plus-sign stitches.

+blue

And because the first spacesuits that went to the moon are historical artifacts, they cannot be taken apart to understand their original pattern or possible deterioration. Conservators initially have to imagine the interiors, to reconstruct + deconstruct the garments seam by seam in their minds. Run the suits backwards through the seamstresses' machines, reverse the fabric one footfall at a time. Rewind each heatproof thread. Uncutting + ungluing + undoing. Eventually, to preserve them, the suits are scanned and X-rayed like a body, to use what bounces back in the images to understand what's coming undone.

I want the garment as it's being crafted and not yet on the moon. I want the collective of women in intimacy in a room, slow sewing all those infinitesimal stitches tailored to suit each body, their seam allowances smaller than the silver glint of an em dash + straight pin accidentally left in. As with many collectives of women who offer an unfathomable but necessary skill, according to the archive, most of us didn't need to know unless there was a need to know. I follow + undo so many threads trying to locate anything anything. I need to know. I want those hours of tracing and cutting and gluing and stitching. The opposite of tearing open a sewn piece of clothing. I want to put my ear directly to the fabric, listen into the impossibly straight airtight lines. Stitch stitch. Are there other grievers out there? Dit dah.

For a long time, what's left of their process exists as the same copied and recirculated images of the women at their long-armed sewing machines, surrounded by billows of silvery mylar or folds and folds of white micrometeoroid fabric. A few showing a glove or boot in construction. I spend hours staring at these photographs, watching the looped footage of the women at work. When I finally stand in front of a real spacesuit, take a self-portrait of my body doubled+ in the mirror of the visor, I have to imagine them gluing each layer, putting in each of the stitches. After endless hours of contacting and searching, a historian from the International Latex Corporation sends me two scanned Polaroids for nonreproducible use. And there they finally are—the seamstresses' card-stock patterns weighed down on a long table, the blue shapes against stark white like the absent areas in lace. And if you look closely, the dotted réseau of pattern-marking paper underneath, a calibration of space.

+twinned

I +

Many of the spacesuits are actually copies. Of which there could be three or more. Every astronaut had a backup, a stress-test suit for use on Earth to simulate the moon + see how well its stitches might hold up, and the suit waiting to head out into space. Often these backups were altered for future use, refitted to another astronaut's body to save time and money. The fabrics are so expensive there's not always enough spacesuits to go around. The first all-female space walk was canceled a few years ago because there weren't enough medium-sized suits for more than one to be worn at a time. So many copies + alterations going round and round that eventually it's difficult to know which are only originals and which are the copies. Each carry in them evidence of the seamstresses.

As the anniversary of the moon landing looms closer + passes there are more and more of the seamstresses' voices to be overheard. New interviews finally recognizing their dazzling handwork. Other footage uncovered. It's years into the future and I'm still listening. As if by eavesdropping on them I am overhearing my mother + my mother's mother + all of the seamstresses in process, talking and sewing and chatting each other up as they piece together a garment across time. Each of us dreaming ourselves into the future in which we can wear our own suits + stop searching for errant pins.

> + —Well when they're up there in space, you know what parts you've worked on and you just say I hope that part don't fail because I'd feel it was my fault if it did.

> + —My sentiment, just what Hazel said, well I just wondered if it was my pair of gloves he had on?

+ —It was that type of a job where you had to go through training, learning how to read blueprints. The way everything was laid out for the way the suits had to be made and everything else.

+ —We were given pieces of fabric that we were supposed to cut into certain sizes and stitch them together and make seams on them and copies of the seams that were projected for the suit.

+ —Every seam you had to make sure you had the right amount of the stitches for that seam so that it could bear the load. And so we had quite a bit to learn.

+ —Every day you get up. You come to work. You go home. You clean house. If you go out there, there's no house, no kids, no problems!

+ —Well, if you put a little stress on it the seam will break. It's not the right kind of seam. It ought to be a turned and overlapped seam.

+ —I'd love to go to space and just live there.

I +

+ In my absence—Rosa, please iron my blackest dress. +

Yes, it is true there is still one dress meant to be worn just once. Just once, this one white dress. And yes, how difficult to have that one dress, meant for just one day, be required to be as exquisite as—. Impossible, really. A bedtime story. Like the one I heard about the daughter who saves herself by requesting a dress the color of the moon, a dress whose dye contains just enough grief to give her strength to leave + the hospital + her wife. Or the childhood story of the Shabbat dress made by her mother that turns from white to black and back again, ruined by soot until the moon's lines touch every dark blot, until the fabric is strewn with beads of light and they glint like pure silver. Or the dress made of a silver-mesh fishing net wrapped round and round so that she is neither clothed nor naked in the moonlight, solving a riddle that leads to her becoming a bride.

To keep people from being tempted to reuse this one dress, we entice a bride-to-be to dazzle herself while facing the unfiltered sunlight, we lure her to wear a color inviting disaster and spills. We tell her stories of Queen Victoria and her attendants wearing white and asking that no other guest wear it—of this day being more valuable than all others, of how all that fabric and stitching and the abundance of hours represents the gravity of standing under the chuppah—crossing the threshold from one life into the next. We don't show her Rovina offstage, changing from one dress into its exact blackest replica. We don't tell her those attendants are all dressed in white to hide the bride from misfortune. We don't tell her until she has a need to know—and even then, she will only know belatedly—that sometimes grief cuts the finishing knot—finds a way of hitching a ride in a seam of a dress as it's being made + transmitted.

How one dress can sit shiva inside another for years.

For these brides, marriage will be more like individual stitches uprooting themselves so slowly—an abundance of hours—that by the time the dress has come undone—sometimes unbeknownst to the wearer—it's best to bury it carefully together.

I +

As long as you can trace the outline of the garment
As long as you are a mother who has recently
As long as your baby did not die before Labor and
Delivery
As long as you are not in inviolate grief + joy
As long as you tear the garment immediately
As long as you have a surviving + original garment
As long as you have a chorus of stitchers + unstitching
As long as your dress is + is not white
As long as you don't leave the straight pins in
As long as you have a garment that has a history of
having been pinned
Pinned open + pinned down + pinned under +
pinned up + pinned together

As long as the text, in its final stages, could not be
folded under a normal sewing machine
As long as there is still dust from the moon in its creases
You can go on round and round
So long as the garment was endless + dazzling to
begin with
So long as the moon is here in the room
So long as there are no signals and notes lost in the
craters + dust
So long as there's no intention to illuminate what's
lost if no longer + twinned
So long as I'm not listening in the pauses and gaps
and hesitation in lace
So long as sometimes looking at Rosa, I + don't
imagine her face

I +

Impossible to wear the garment in process + in between acts—the fabric before + after it is done + undone, flat and not yet patterned + repatterned. A garment suspended in the speculative future. Future garment + surviving garment. I am choosing not to choose which garment will be made + unmade.

No final garment + footage to capture the treading—treading—through a room full of incubators and exhausted parents trying to locate—every day for days + months—no moon in the room—are there any grievers out there? Or the resilience of these preemies in their moon suits, wrinkled up inside. Or walking out on my original due date ten weeks later—both + two of us alive.

If there were documentary photographs they would be of the moon in process—waxing and waning—depending on which way you entered the exhibit. In the final photograph, only one fully crystallized child. And for every year ahead, a ghost of the same age made of salt drifting + dreaming at the bottom of the lake. Too heavy to lift whole from the water.

Every year I tell you every year we celebrate Rosa having gone round and round and I put up a large banner that says: —HAPPY BIRTHDAY UNOFFICIALLY ROSA—

She would have been Rosa if her name had not been Rosa. She would have been Rosa if she had been a twin.

Rosa is her name is her name.

I +

Spring in a new house, some new city, again. New year, year—how to separate you from the wind? Dust from the moon under the sofa. All morning your sisters sprawled across the living room floor writing a play. Again there are costumes, and a script, and other bits of preparation. This endless Earth plague still incubating us, our loneliness, pressing our faces to the glass—so each of their parts will have to be cast from somewhere inside this house. And every time, inexplicably, a third role written that requires another child. One that can't + didn't come in. Again and again an empty role. An empty role and a moon + a red balloon hanging its grief in the corner of the room. + But if I put on a white dress and go out, I will be lost in the light and lost again—and how will I find the spring in your absence?

When the daughter's Shabbat dress turns from white to black to the moon's silver glint, her mother doesn't recognize her as she walks home all aglow—*Who is this?* And the daughter runs to her, laughing—*Do you not recognize me?* And the daughter tells her everything that has happened—that will happen—that will never be—and they return home together—her dress filling every room—lighting the whole house. Until she disappears back out into the night sky.

O + hospital spring—in this century + of grief and the next and the next. Where + are you hiding in this wide-open brightness? Perhaps I will race through + a new future—me in black and you in + white, me with a + pair of flowers in my hair, you with a thousand + congratulatory flowers in yours, which is how we will recognize each other. I will be the only possible me—. Just in case, I will carry + my mother's heavy silver sewing scissors in one hand and, in the other, + the last whispered hush you might have heard—you will recognize me by my handkerchief + ready to plant in the dust on the moon, for you—in the midst of this empty sky, which I breathe in and breathe in—you will be the only possible you—I will recognize you— + by the threads of our dresses.

+ Rose is a rose is a rose is a rose. +

Goodnight +nobody

+somebody

| +

+ Dickinson is also choosing not to choose between the suggestion that certain experiences can be mapped—can be made comprehensible in terms of geographies and exteriors—and the suggestion made by the same poems that such experiences cannot be. +

Difficult to know when entering the artist's exhibit who is playing the "Moonlight Sonata." The starless grand piano angled so it's unclear whether the keys are being pressed by the hands of a performer or if the notes—moonlight glinting on the dark surface of a lake—are floating off on their own through the space. It's the same black piano found in hospital lobbies, the music trailing visitors and patients into the elevators, inviting them to imagine they are arriving + returning somewhere else. Some other future. Cross the room and it's clear that nobody is playing this moonlight. Its lullaby recognizable even as we hear something is suspended + torn as it goes round and round. The artist wants us to imagine only the moon and its sonic negative are present in this room—rising slowly across the blank sky of the gallery's white walls as the music undoes itself again and again. The lost notes gathering as patterns + absence. Goodnight moon + Goodnight moon + And— + And— + And—

+ What is a variant + if not the refusal of an epitaph's eternal concision + the opposite of a monument—with its haughty typography + a variant is an expansion—+ a going-on-forever—+ a text + dress reanimated revived again and again in the act of revision + alteration + repair + the fine-tuning of its fabric + a variant calibrates + is a pause + miraculously safe + invents an interior, an elsewhere + is embroidered, unembroidered + escapes the circle + escapes repetition + is a record + is a light + a lamp + a template + a navigation + a means of transport + loses sight of the moon, of us + all together—turn the dress and the folded seam splits it into an open-winged bird—+ turn it again and the pattern of stitches takes you across another horizon entirely +

+ +

— +

—+ —+ +

+ + +

+ + +

+ +

+ +

+ + +

+ + +

+ + —

—+

+

WORKS CITED

Valerie Mendes quoting Pierre Cardin, *Pierre Cardin: Past, Present, Future* + Kaat Debo, *Patronen: Patterns* + Nicholas de Monchaux, *Spacesuit: Fashioning Apollo* + NASA seamstresses, *Moonwalk One* + Hettie Judah, "An Artist's Salt Crystal Gown, Created Deep Under the Dead Sea" + Christopher Jobson quoting Sigalit Landau, "A 19th Century Dress Submerged in the Dead Sea Becomes Gradually Crystallized with Salt" + Emily Dickinson, *Envelope Poems* + Margaret Wise Brown, *Goodnight Moon* + Caroline Evans, "Capturing the Ghost," *Exploding Fashion: Making, Unmaking, and Remaking Twentieth-Century Fashion* + Katie Paterson, *Earth-Moon-Earth (Moonlight Sonata Reflected from the Surface of the Moon)* + Margaret Wise Brown, *The Color Kittens* + Shahidha Bari, "Capturing the Ghost,"

Exploding Fashion: Making, Unmaking, and Remaking Twentieth-Century Fashion + Daneen Wardrop, *Emily Dickinson and the Labor of Clothing* + Patricia Cowings, *Space for Women* + Annette Duburg/Rixt van der Trol, *Draping: Art and Craftsmanship in Fashion Design* + Ingrid Mida/Alexandra Kim, *The Dress Detective: A Practical Guide to Object-Based Research in Fashion* + Roland Barthes, *The Fashion System* + Gertrude Stein, "Sacred Emily" + Emily Dickinson, *The Poems of Emily Dickinson: Reading Edition* + E. B. White, "Comment" (July 18, 1969) + Gertrude Stein, *The World Is Round* + Emily Dickinson, *The Master Letters of Emily Dickinson* + Gertrude Stein, *Counting Her Dresses: A Play* + Jenny Erpenbeck, *Visitation* + Rabbi Kenneth Berger, "Five Minutes to Live" + Margaret Atwood, *The Handmaid's Tale* + Nicholas Alfrey, "Transmission, Reflection and Loss: Katie Paterson's Earth-Moon-Earth" + Elizabeth Dye interviewed by Avery Trufelman, "Wedding Dresses: *Articles of Interest* #12" + Sarah Goff-Dupont quoting Jean Wright, "Stitches in Space: The Astronaut's Clothes" + Arthur Russell, "This Is How We Walk on the Moon" + Strong Golisano Children's Hospital NICU website + Liz Stinson quoting Cathy Lewis, "X-Rays Reveal the Insane Innards of Space Suits"

+ Caring Hands for Angels website + Clarice Lispector, "Spring Suite Swiss-Style" + Itzhak Schweiger-Dmi'el, *Hanna's Sabbath Dress* + Sharon Cameron, *Choosing Not Choosing* + Anne Dufourmantelle, "Risking Variation"

ACKNOWLEDGMENTS

+ In memory of Madeline (Midge) Wood—
for teaching me to alter

& Jed Deppman—for giving me Dickinson

The writing of this book was made possible by fellowships from the Tanner Humanities Center and the Lawrence T. and Janet T. Dee Foundation as well as a Western Washington University summer research award. With special thanks to the Taft-Nicholson Environmental Humanities Center.

An early interactive version of this essay appeared on Territory (themapisnot.com) as "Variants on the Moon" and was chosen as a notable essay in *The Best American Essays 2020*. Thank you to Thomas Mira y Lopez and Nick Greer for inviting me to write for the twins issue.

Wild thanks to Adam and Ashley Levy and Transit Books for seeing the seed of this essay and believing in it, with incredible patience as it unfolded during a pandemic. What an honor to work with you. Lizzie Davis—you are the dream editor + the ideal reader. Thank you for the light of your gorgeous mind.

Stefania Heim—thank you for your sharp eyes and unwavering belief in choosing not to choose.

To all the NICU nurses at Strong Memorial Hospital in Rochester, NY—especially and always Amy Szymanowicz—there will never be gratitude enough. And to Stefania Uticone for sharing those final weeks.

Noam Dorr—love + editing is happening.

SV and RC, the incredible -tines siblings—for everything, and—

CORI WINROCK is a poet and multimedia essayist. Her most recent book, *Little Envelope of Earth Conditions*, was chosen as Editor's Choice for the Alice James Book Award. She is the winner of the Boston Review Poetry Prize, and her essay on twins was selected as a notable essay in *The Best American Essays 2020*. Her work has appeared in *POETRY*, the *Best New Poets* anthology, *Bennington Review*, *West Branch*, *Fairy Tale Review*, and elsewhere. She is an assistant professor of interactive poetics at Western Washington University.

UNDELIVERED LECTURES is a narrative nonfiction series featuring book-length essays in slim, handsome editions.

01 Mary Cappello, *Lecture*
02 Namwali Serpell, *Stranger Faces*
03 Mariana Oliver, *Migratory Birds*
04 Preti Taneja, *Aftermath*
05 Joanna Walsh, *My Life as a Godard Movie*
06 Ayşegül Savaş, *The Wilderness*
07 Lauren Markham, *Immemorial*
08 Iman Mersal, *Motherhood and Its Ghosts*
09 Cori Winrock, *Alterations*

Transit Books is a nonprofit publisher of international and American literature, based in Berkeley, California. Founded in 2015, Transit Books is committed to the discovery and promotion of enduring works that carry readers across borders and communities. Visit us online to learn more about our forthcoming titles, events, and opportunities to support our mission.

TRANSITBOOKS.ORG